Table of Contents

Prologue 6
    Khomeini's Caliphate 7
    Guardian Council 9
    Presidency 10
    Spiritual and Practical Allegiance to the Supreme Leader 11
    The Assembly of Experts 12

Chapter 1: Basic Facts on Parliamentary
and Assembly of Experts Elections 16
    Historical Background: The Fundamental Contradiction of the
        Iranian Regime with the Concept of Elections 16
    The Composition of the Regime's Parliament 18
    The number of electoral districts and ballot boxes in Iran 19
    Elections Processes and Deadlines 20
    Main Agencies Involved in the Iranian Regime's Elections 22
    A: Interior Ministry 22
    The Elections Committee 23
    Elections Supervisory Body (Interior Ministry) 24
    Central Elections Investigations Office (Interior Ministry) 24
    Elections Monitors and Observers 24
    Elections Administrators 25
    The Interior Ministry's Vetting Process 25

Comparative Statistics of the 10 parliamentary
    elections and Interior Ministry disqualifications 26
Approval Rates by the Interior
    Ministry for the past 10 election cycles: 27
B: The Guardian Council 28
Composition of the Guardian Council 29
Guardian Council's Electoral Authorities 29
"Approbation Supervision" (Nezarat-e Estesvabi) 30
Supervisory Offices of the Guardian Council 31
Members of the Central Electoral
    Supervisory Office (Guardian Council) 32
IRGC Intelligence Organization:
    Guardian Council's Main Instrument 33
The Purge and Disqualifications by the
    Guardian Council in the Current Parliamentary Election 34
All Candidates and Disqualifications
    in 31 Provinces for the 10th Parliamentary Elections 36
Past Disqualifications by the
    Guardian Council for Parliamentary Elections 38
Past Disqualifications Chart
    by the Guardian Council for Parliamentary Elections 39
Election Funding and the Illicit Role o
    f the Iranian Regime's Organizations 41
Using Drug Money to Pay for Campaigns 41
Political Parties within the Regime 44
The "Reformist" Faction and Its Electoral Tactics 46
The "Principalists" (pro-Khamenei)
    Faction and Electoral Tactics 49
Participation of Women 53

Chapter 2: Analysis of the 2016 Elections 55
    Engineering of Election Results by Khamenei 55
    Background 55
    Reasons for Escalation of Infighting
        on the Brink of the Elections... 58
    Rafsanjani-Rouhani Take
        Their Fight to the Guardian Council............................. 59
    Khamenei Personally Manipulates Elections...................... 62
    Meeting of IRGC Commanders on
        Engineering Election Results 67
    Fear of Popular Protests: Main Factor
        Behind the Regime's Decisions
        for Upcoming Elections.. 67
    Decisions by the Supreme
        National Security Council
        on the Eve of the Elections.. 67

Prologue

Iranian regime's Parliament (Majlis)

The Iranian regime holds elections for the presidency, parliament (*Majlis*), Assembly of Experts, and municipal councils. Yet this jumbled appearance of a representative government can deceive the western eye. The clerical regime has a contradictory nature, uncharacteristic of any theocracy that has ruled before it: seemingly holding elections while effectively preserving a monopoly of power through the "supreme leader". That institution represents the essence of its undemocratic nature.

The clerical regime came into power after the anti-monarchical revolution of 1979, which overthrew the Shah's dictatorship. The Iranian people had succeeded in generating one of the most inspiring revolutions of the 20th century. The popular sentiment at the time clearly leaned towards a democratic and pluralistic government representative of Iran's ethnic, social and religious mosaic. This attitude had been a formative underlying theme in Iran's politics since the 1906 constitutional revolution. Still, the Iranian people did not have a well-known democratic alternative that could replace the Shah.

Enter Khomeini and his religious fundamentalists. Under the watchful eye of the Shah, democratic activists were imprisoned, tortured and murdered while religious fundamentalists flourished openly, building hundreds of mosques and expanding their organizational and financial networks. Relying on his social apparatus, Khomeini used foreign channels and backroom deals with the military and other elements of the Shah's regime to essentially hijack the revolution. Instead of a democratic government, he began to establish a theocratic order by concentrating the state apparatus in the hands of a few clerics. The Iranian people's democratic revolution was commandeered and falsely rebranded as the "Islamic Revolution" to serve Khomeini's purposes.

Khomeini's Caliphate

Since the 1940s, decades before the advent of the group currently calling itself the Islamic State (ISIS/ISIL) and other extremist terrorist groups, Khomeini had openly advocated the establishment of an Islamic caliphate that extended beyond Iran's recognized borders. When he hijacked the revolution, Khomeini faced major popular resistance to his efforts to implement his radical ideas. Instead, he was forced to tame his ambitions to placate a progressive society.

He acquiesced to having a "president" and creating a "parliament," which he later renamed as the "Islamic Consultative Assembly."

Assembly of Experts

The mullahs crafted a constitution that included "elections" and hazy visages of a republic, but they robbed these institutions of any major practical influence. Today, these outwardly democratic institutions are checked by a shadow system of clergy-dominated institutions. Within the narrow confines of an ideologically backward religious fundamentalist state, they control elections and governance. That is why "elected" officials in Iran are subservient to the supreme leader and are hardly regarded as representatives of the majority of the population, who remain alienated from the political order. The main avenue for the Iranian populace to express itself politically is through protests and uprisings, which are brutally suppressed by the regime.

Guardian Council

Central to any election in Iran is a managing and supervisory body called the Guardian Council (*Shora-ye Negahban*), whose members are vetted by, and subservient to, the supreme leader. According to the constitution, all candidates in all elections in Iran must be vetted and approved by the Guardian Council (under the auspices of the supreme leader). The Guardian Council routinely disqualifies most candidates who run for office - even within the already narrow confines of the theocracy. In 2009, for instance, out of the 476 candidates for presidency, many of whom were and still are loyal regime officials, only four were allowed to run.

Elections in such a system, where an unelected leader picks the candidates and says "now choose," cannot escape a thick and palpable air of illegitimacy. The filtered elected officials are thus strictly devoted to an illegitimate regime and specifically to an unelected supreme leader.

What is more, the Guardian Council's selection criteria have proven to be vague and arbitrary. Indeed, at times, candidates who have previously served the regime for years and whose candidacies were approved repeatedly in the past by the same body can face surprising disqualifications on seemingly arbitrary grounds. Perhaps the most famous example was that of Ali Akbar Hashemi Rafsanjani, who even as his candidacy for president was rejected in 2009, is a former president of eight years and was at the time presiding over the powerful Exigency Council, which has oversight on the actions of the president.

Ali Akbar Hashemi Rafsanjani

Although they play an instrumental role in short-listing candidates, the members of the Guardian Council themselves are not elected. The 12-member body is comprised of six clerics, all of whom are handpicked by the supreme leader, and six lawyers, who are recommended by the judiciary (whose head is appointed by the supreme leader) and approved by parliament. In addition to supervising elections, the unelected Council has enormous legislative authority with an ability to veto any parliament legislation that it deems unconstitutional or contrary to Sharia law.

Presidency

The president of the Iranian regime, although ostensibly elected by the people, must answer to the supreme leader. In fact, even after the people elect the president, the supreme leader is still constitutionally empowered to reject him (based on the constitutional principle of *tanfiz*). Notably, women and ethnic and religious minorities are not qualified to run for president at all. (The constitution uses the Arabic word 'rejal' or men as a legal means to ban women.)

Spiritual and Practical Allegiance to the Supreme Leader

Importantly, all candidates who stand for elections must demonstrate "spiritual and practical allegiance" to the supreme leader and the theocratic regime (*velayat-e faqih*).

Much like other dictatorships, in practice, the regime has not relied on "elections" as a genuine conduit for the free expression of public sentiment. Rather, it has exploited elections as a means to legitimize its own illegitimate hold on power. Voting is mandatory for many state employees and elections are routinely marred by accusations of widespread fraud and irregularities.

Still, the supreme leader wants to use elections as a means to legitimize his hold on power. On January 20, 2016, the state-run TV quoted Khamenei as saying, "even those who oppose the Islamic Republic should take part in the election. (But) this does not mean that opponents of the Islamic Republic should be elected."

Ali Larijani, Speaker of Parliament

"Only those who believe in the Islamic Republic and its values should be allowed to enter parliament," he added. Which raises the question: why would anyone opposed to the regime, want to vote if his or her preferred candidates are not allowed to run?

The Assembly of Experts

The Assembly of Experts (*Majlis-e Khobregan-e Rahbari*) is comprised of 88 clerics who serve eight-year terms. The Assembly's official mandate is to supervise, appoint or dismiss the Iranian regime's supreme leader, currently Ali Khamenei. In reality, however, the body is hardly a real check against the supreme leader's powers and has never seriously questioned his authority. One reason is that the election system requires the candidates to have "spiritual and practical allegiance" to the supreme leader. The supreme leader's appointees must approve all candidates, including those running for the Assembly of Experts.

Crucial election of Assembly of Experts

Every year, the Assembly of Experts holds two closed-door sessions. The people and even the state-run media are not privy to the discussions carried out among the 88 mullahs. At times, some topics of discussion are publicized only in the most general format. Ironically, then, the people who purportedly elect the members of the Assembly of Experts hardly know what these members do after they are elected.

More peculiarly, the members of the Assembly of Experts, who ostensibly monitor the supreme leader's actions, have to be indirectly approved by the supreme leader himself. Prior to standing for elections, the candidates must be approved by the Guardian Council, whose six clerics are directly appointed by the supreme leader, thus giving him control over who can stand for elections in the Assembly of Experts in the first place.

Hassan Khomeini registers his candidacy for the forthcoming elections to the Assembly of Experts in Tehran

After the 1979 revolution, the newly established regime drafted a constitution that granted ultimate power to the *vali-e faqih*, at the time Khomeini himself. Nearly four months after taking power, Khomeini broke his earlier promises about an inclusive and truly representative constituent assembly and instead opted to create an assembly made up exclusively of clerics (calling it the Assembly of Experts). The aim was to create a formal mechanism to regulate succession of power and thus to preserve his "Islamic State" through successive caliphs.

After Khomeini's death, which was kept a secret for several days, his successor Khamenei was quickly appointed by the Assembly of Experts in 1989 even though he did not qualify for the position, primarily in order to prevent popular uprisings against a leaderless and vulnerable illegitimate regime.

Today, although different factions of the regime jockey for positions within the Assembly during elections, according to the constitution, the supreme leader yields the most power within the theocracy. According to Article 110, he must approve the regime's general policies. As the commander-in-chief of the armed forces, he appoints commanders of military and security forces as well as the commander of the Islamic Revolutionary Guard Corps (IRGC). He also handpicks the head of the regime's main broadcast network (the Islamic Republic of Iran Broadcasting, or IRIB) as well as the head of the judiciary. He is in charge of all state security apparatuses and has the final say on all major domestic and foreign policy decisions.

Since the Assembly of Experts was effectively designed by the mullahs to circumvent the establishment of an inclusive constituent assembly (as the Iranian people demanded), it is seen as an institution that symbolizes the usurping of power by fundamentalist clerics. Therefore, it lacks fundamental legitimacy that citizens usually afford to sovereign governments.

The rival factions who pose as "moderates" or "reformists" seek a larger piece of the political and economic pie usurped from the Iranian people by the regime in its entirety. They have no plans to include the Iranian people in political decision-making. They have no designs for democracy, because that would undermine the entire system, introducing irreparable cracks in the wall of suppression and dictatorship. Hassan Rouhani- as a pillar of the regime - is just as loyal to Khamenei's office as Khamenei's most ardent supporters.

Iranian regime's President Hassan Rouhani

Importantly, half of the Iranian population, women, have been excluded from critical elements of the election process a fact in and of itself indicative that the current state of affairs is unsustainable. It will not be the regime "moderates" who introduce genuine change. That task has fallen on the millions of disenfranchised, especially the younger generation who comprise 70 percent of the population, who seek democracy, tolerance and a secular republic that respects human rights, gender equality, and popular sovereignty. The Iranian people know full well that until such change, elections in Iran are not a genuine avenue for their representation in the political sphere. Elections are simply another forum for various elements of the ruling dictatorship to gain more power and influence, which the rulers will then translate into domestic suppression, terrorism, and export of Islamic fundamentalism.

Chapter 1: Basic Facts on Parliamentary and Assembly of Experts Elections

Historical Background: The Fundamental Contradiction of the Iranian Regime with the Concept of Elections

Elections in the context of the absolute clerical rule (*velayat-e faqih*) in Iran are, in fact, a well-orchestrated farce, a sham designed to deceive the Iranian people and international community into thinking that the various appointments of the "caliph" (supreme leader) actually occur through open elections by the people.

The difference between an "Islamic State" and the Iranian regime is that in the former, the "caliph" overtly installs individuals in various posts, while the Iranian regime's supreme leader offers several completely subservient candidates of his choosing to the voters, thus giving the illusion of choice. For example, he accepts several individuals for the presidency, often one or two candidates for each seat in the Assembly of Experts, and several candidates for each parliamentary seat. But they are all vetted through an extremely reactionary body called the Guardian Council.

In the next act of this deceptive performance, "elections" are kicked into full gear when various factions within the regime enter the race in support of different candidates vetted by the supreme leader and considered loyal to the dictatorship.

In subsequent stages, after the candidates register and officially enter the fray, factional feuding escalates as different groups within the regime vie for more power and state resources. Elections, then, are simply a thin coat of paint on an otherwise undemocratic process guarded and at times engineered by the unelected supreme leader.

A cursory review of the Iranian regime's constitution itself can shed some light on the true characteristics of elections within the regime:

- **Article 91:** "With a view to safeguarding the Islamic ordinances and the Constitution, in order to examine the compatibility of the legislation passed by the Islamic Consultative Assembly [Parliament] with Islam, a council to be known as the Guardian Council is to be constituted. …"

- **Article 93:** "The Islamic Consultative Assembly [Parliament] does not hold any legal status if there is no Guardian Council in existence. …"

- **Article 99:** "The Guardian Council has the responsibility of supervising the elections of the Assembly of Experts for Leadership, the President of the Republic, the Islamic

Consultative Assembly, and the direct recourse to popular opinion and referenda."

Such self-made state organs have seen their authority expanded over the past 37 years, preserving the supreme leader's power alongside the Islamic Revolutionary Guard Corps (IRGC) against the will of the Iranian people. According to a *fatwa* or a religious decree issued by the regime's previous supreme leader Khomeini, "the system's preservation trumps all other duties," and anything that the regime does or refrains from doing can be viewed in this context.

It can be clearly seen, then, that the *velayat-e faqih* dictatorship in Iran, in addition to the specific articles of the constitution solidifying the authority of the supreme leader against the popular will, has in practice created its own unique organs and institutions like the Assembly of Experts, the Guardian Council and the Exigency Council to bolster and preserve the role of the supreme leader in the regime.

The Composition of the Regime's Parliament

The tenth round of elections for the parliament and the fifth for the Assembly of Experts will be held simultaneously on February 26, 2016. There are 290 seats up for grabs in the parliament, whose deputies will serve a four-year term. The parliamentary election will be in two stages, with the second stage, taking place in May 2016. The new parliament will officially convene on May 27, 2016.

For the 2016 elections, there are 12,123 registered candidates, 1,461 of whom are women.

Factional feuding in Iranian regime's Majlis

Votes are counted manually, primarily in order to facilitate fraud. For the 2016 elections, weary of having his preferred candidates lose because of fraud committed by rival factions, Hassan Rouhani's government held lengthy discussions with the Guardian Council to propose an electronic system of vote counting. But the Guardian Council ultimately shot down his administration's proposal on January 20, 2016.

The number of electoral districts and ballot boxes in Iran

According to the latest official statistics (2015), the total population of Iran is 79,020,100.

There are a total of 207 electoral districts (with 1,633 centers)

There are a total 60,000 polling stations in the country, with an estimated 110,000 ballot boxes.

The number of polling stations in Tehran province exceeds 6,400.

The statistics on the population should be viewed in the context of a prevalent fraudulent scheme by the regime that leads to widespread irregularity in each election. Official figures reduce the real population by approximately seven million people in order to increase the participation rate.

Elections Processes and Deadlines

Steps	Timelines
Orders issued to members of the elections committee	April 12, 2015
Order to commence elections process for the 10th Parliament and 5th Assembly of Experts	December 11, 2015
Formation of the executive action committee for the 5th Assembly of Experts	December 12, 2015 - December 17, 2015
Formation of the executive action committee for the 10th Islamic Consultative Assembly (parliament)	December 19, 2015 - December 25, 2015

Registration period for the 10th Islamic Consultative Assembly (parliament)	December 15, 2015 - December 25, 2015
Registration period for the 5th Assembly of Experts	December 17, 2015 - December 23, 2015
Vetting process and background checks on candidates for the 10th parliament (by the executive action committees as well as the Ministry of Intelligence, State Security Forces, Registry Office and the Judiciary)	December 19, 2015 - December 29, 2015
Opportunity for those disqualified to appeal	January 6, 2016 - January 9, 2016
Guardian Council's review of appeals and complaints	February 9, 2016 - February 15, 2016
Start of campaigning for the 5th Assembly of Experts	February 11, 2016 - February 24, 2016
Start of campaigning for the 10th parliament	February 18, 2016 - February 24, 2016
End of campaign period for both parliament and Assembly of Experts	February 25, 2016
Election day	February 26, 2016

Main Agencies Involved in the Iranian Regime's Elections

A: Interior Ministry

Since the outset of the Iranian regime's establishment in 1979, the dominant faction in charge of the Interior Ministry has tried to sideline or push out other factions by controlling the vetting process.

Will Ali Larijani remain as Speaker of Parliament

Since Hassan Rouhani took the presidency in 2013, the Interior Ministry has been in the hands of factions allied with him and the current parliamentary speaker Ali Larijani. In accordance with their faction's overall policy, the Interior Ministry has accepted the candidacy of most applicants for the 2016 elections, thus leaving the final political decision to the Guardian Council.

A cursory look at the affiliations of the elections committee members and statistics around the candidates whose applications were rejected demonstrates this fact.

The Elections Committee

- Interior Ministry headed by Interior Minister Abdol-Reza Rahmani Fazli, affiliated with the Rouhani-Larijani faction
- Head of the Elections Committee: Moqimi, the Deputy Interior Minister and apolitical advisor
- Seyyed Alireza Avai: Head of the Registry Office and member of the Elections Committee
- Seyyed Shahaboddin Chavoshi: Head of Tehran Province's Political and Social Affairs and Chair of the Tehran Province Elections Committee

On April 19, 2015, the following Interior Ministry officials were appointed to the Elections Committee while being allowed to keep their primary jobs:

- Hossein-Ali Amiri, deputy minister in charge of legislative and provincial affairs; member of the committee;
- Hossein Zolfaqari, deputy minister in charge of security and disciplinary affairs; member, and head of the security and disciplinary division of the Elections Committee;
- Javad Nasserian, deputy minister in charge of resource and management development: head of the financial and logistics office of the Elections Committee;
- Seyyed Salman Samani, chair of the center for investigative actions and legal affairs: head of the legal office of the Elections Committee;
- Amir Shoja'an, chair of the center for government technological advancement: member and head of the IT

department of the Elections Committee;
- Mohammad Ebrahim Shoushtari, advisor to the minister and head of the security team: head of the Committee's security
- Varali Motlaq and Babak Dinparast: Secretary and Communications Lead of the Elections Committee;

Elections Supervisory Body (Interior Ministry)

Members are Mullah Ebrahimi, Qassem Mohammad Tehran, Farhad Rahbar, Mohammad-Hossein Sadequ, and Gholam-Hossein Ebrahimi.

Central Elections Investigations Office (Interior Ministry)

Seyyed Salman Samani, chair of the center for investigative actions and legal affairs, is also the head of the elections investigations office.

Elections Monitors and Observers

Hamed Shayan, head of the public relations office of the Tehran Province Elections Monitoring and Investigations Office; Mullah Seyyed Abdolvahab Ashrafi, chair of the Elections Monitors; Hadi Nour-Mohammad, member; Ali-Asqar Jokar, member.

Elections Administrators

There are somewhere between 1.2 to 1.3 million election administrators, excluding executive committee members. They are primarily tied to the IRGC, the Bassij Force and other security and military organs. These election administrators are essentially responsible for preventing social protests and uprisings, controlling ballot boxes and preparing them for elections fraud and engineered outcomes.

The Interior Ministry's Vetting Process

Subsequent to the registration of the candidates, all of whom, in accordance with the regime's constitution, must display "loyalty to the supreme leader, both spiritually and in practice," the vetting process and settling of factional scores begins. The candidates are first accepted or rejected by the Interior Ministry's executive committee on the basis of reports from four other bodies: The Ministry of Intelligence, the State Security Forces, the Judiciary and the Registry Office. The lists of accepted and rejected candidates are then passed on to the Guardian Council for further review.

During the 2016 elections, the Rouhani faction in the Interior Ministry approved the candidacies of a large number of candidates in line with its tactics to control more seats in parliament and in the Assembly of Experts. It wanted to lay the groundwork for discrediting the Guardian Council, which is controlled by the rival pro-Khamenei faction, forcing it to reject a large number of candidates.

The Interior Ministry spokesman, Hossein-Ali Amiri, announced after the vetting of the candidates: Out of a total of 12,123 people who registered for elections of the Islamic Consultative Assembly, 10,954 were approved and 814 were disqualified by the executive committees of the country.

Comparative Statistics of the 10 parliamentary elections and Interior Ministry disqualifications

No.	Elections Date	# of Withdrawn Candidacies	No announcements	Approved	Disqualified	Total	% approved	% disqualified
1	March 14, 1980	68	2691	531	415	3748	14.16	11.07
2	April 15, 1984	141	52	1144	253	1590	71.94	15.91
3	April 8, 1988	51	899	823	200	1994	41.27	10.03
4	April 10, 1992	304	213	1876	853	3276	57.26	26.03
5	March 8, 1996	253	17	2837	2246	5361	52.91	41.89
6	Feb 8, 2000	1095	17	5350	386	6852	78.07	5.63
7	April 1, 2003	1354	34	6340	422	8167	77.62	5.16
8	March 14, 2008	808	17	4458	1907	7595	58.69	25.1
9	March 2, 2012	474	3	3541	851	5382	65.79	15.81
10	Feb 26, 2016	266	31	10901	790	12050	90.46	6.55

Approval Rates by the Interior Ministry for the past 10 election cycles:

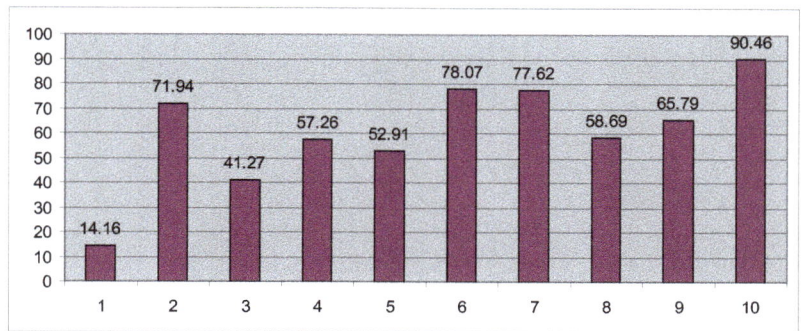

Looking at the numbers in the table above, it can be seen that this elections cycle has had the most candidates approved by the Interior Ministry (execution action committees), with a 90.46% approval rate.

The least number of approvals occurred in the first round of parliamentary elections, with 14.16%.

During the presidency of Ali Akbar Hashemi Rafsanjani (1989-1997), an average of 50% of candidates were approved.

Hassan Rouhani and Ali Akbar Hashemi Rafsanjani

During the presidency of Mohammad Khatami (1997-2005), an average of 77% of candidates were approved.

As mentioned above, the differences among the percentage of candidates approved or disqualified during the various periods reveals the general political bent of the Interior Ministry at that point in time, i.e. its plan to eliminate other factions while paving the way for its candidates.

Both the pro-Khamenei and the so-called "reformist" camps use fraud and other tools at their disposal to grab more power and access to oil revenues. Neither the "reformists" nor the "hardliners" care that the Iranian people are by and large excluded from the entire process. When it comes to the fundamental tenets of the religious tyrannical system, all factions within the regime share the same undemocratic objectives and values.

B: The Guardian Council

The Guardian Council is a key organ in the *velayat-e faqih* regime, entrusted with protecting the "Islamic State" (caliphate). The idea of creating the Guardian Council came from Khomeini himself. Following the 1979 revolution, the ruling clerics ratified three principles for the formation of the Guardian Council and its authorities as a means of solidifying and ensuring the continuation of their reactionary beliefs.

The Guardian Council officially began work on July 16, 1980. Since then, it has fulfilled its two main responsibilities: reviewing parliamentary bills to determine inconsistencies with Sharia law and the regime's constitution, and vetting and supervising elections in the theocratic system.

Composition of the Guardian Council

The Guardian Council has 12 members who serve for six years. They include six clerics and six jurists. Based on the constitution, the supreme leader appoints the six clerics and can re-appoint them as well. Ahmad Jannati, the current chairman, has been a member of the Guardian Council for the past 36 years.

The six jurists are nominated by the judiciary and later approved by parliament. Since the supreme leader, in practice appoints the judiciary's head, all 12 members of the Guardian Council are either directly or indirectly appointed by the supreme leader.

Guardian Council's Electoral Authorities

Mullah Ahmad Jannati, who for a significant portion of his 36 years in office has been the chairman, officially stated in 2007 that the Guardian Council's responsibility is to "prevent impious people from attaining positions of power."

In addition to reviewing parliamentary legislation to determine inconsistencies with Sharia law and the regime's undemocratic constitution, the Guardian Council also supervises and decides on the competency of all electoral candidates.

According to Article 69 of the constitution, parliamentary "legislation passed at a closed session is valid only ... in the presence of the Guardian Council."

And, Article 98 of the constitution reads, "The authority of the interpretation of the Constitution is vested with the Guardian Council."

"Approbation Supervision" (Nezarat-e Estesvabi)

In May 1991, simultaneous with the fourth round of parliamentary elections, then-chairman of the Guardian Council, Mohammad Mohammadi Gilani, said that the supervisory authority outlined in article 99 of the constitution is approbatory (i.e. formal approval or rejection) and includes "all of the electoral stages, including approving or disqualifying of candidates." As such, in addition to having the authority of general and comprehensive supervision over elections since 1991 the Guardian Council has maintained complete authority over the approval or rejection of the candidates in elections for the Assembly of Experts, parliament, and presidency.

The extent of its authority is such that it does not deem it necessary nor is it prepared to explain the context and criteria for its decisions. As a result, there have been cases where the candidacy of the same person has been approved and rejected in a very short span of time.

Again, despite their rivalries, all of the regime's officials and factions are genuinely in agreement when it comes to the pillars of the theocracy, including the Guardian Council and the supreme leader. On December 19, 2015, Rouhani's Interior Minister Abdol-Reza Rahmani Fazli said during a televised interview: "I support the principle of approbation supervision 100 percent because it is law and one cannot act against it."

Hassan Rouhani, Ali Akbar Hashemi Rafsanjani, Ali Khamenei

The rivalry between Khamenei and other factions is not over genuine reforms or acceding to popular demand or democracy. At its core, the factional rivalry is over access to power and financial resources.

Supervisory Offices of the Guardian Council

Before Mohammad Khatami became the regime's president in 1997, supreme leader Ali Khamenei's faction centrally controlled all of the security, intelligence, and judicial bodies. The Guardian Council, too, belonged to that faction as a lever and main tool for rejecting candidates who showed even a semblance of disagreement with Khamenei's positions.

With the ascent of Khatami and the resulting internal bipolarity, especially after revelations about the murder of dissidents during an episode that later became known as the "chain killings" of the 1990s, many of Khamenei's agents were sacked from the Intelligence Ministry (some had ties to the murders). Consequently, the pro-Khamenei factions created their own shadow intelligence ministry.

Regardless, the Guardian Council could no longer rely as heavily on the official Intelligence Ministry. In 2001, the Guardian Council set up and later expanded a new organization called the "Supervisory Office" in provincial capitals and other cities. By 2013, on the brink of the presidential elections, the number of Guardian Council observers had reached 385,000.

Members of the Central Electoral Supervisory Office (Guardian Council)

Mohammad Reza Aref

Members of the Central Electoral Supervisory Office include: mullah Ahmad Jannati (chairman), mullah Mohammad Yazdi (deputy), Mohammad-Reza Alizadeh (secretary), Siamak Rahpeyk (spokesman), and mullah Seyyed Ebrahim Raeesi. All are close to Khamenei and have played a significant role in the suppression of the Iranian people.

IRGC Intelligence Organization: Guardian Council's Main Instrument

Following the 2009 uprisings, the IRGC's Intelligence Organization was formed with the intent of suppressing any and all popular uprisings. Its head is mullah Hossein Taib.

The organization is comprised of 10 departments, four of which are the primary bodies: intelligence gathering, political office, social office, and security office. The intelligence-gathering arm has an extensive network of spies and agents organized by the Bassij Force. They gather information from all social sectors and branches, including universities, government institutions, manufacturing plants, mosques and various city districts. This department then communicates the intelligence it has gathered on the ground to the other three primary departments (political, social and security).

The political department, which has an active relationship during elections with the Guardian Council's supervisory office, is itself divided into the three branches of "political parties," "universities," and regime "officials and managers."

The "political parties" branch is active in the surveillance of all parties, including those tied to the Khamenei faction, "reformists," other groups and non-governmental organizations (NGOs).

The "universities" branch is engaged in the surveillance of post-secondary students and student organizations.

The "officials and managers" branch monitors regime officials, both junior and senior, serving in the executive, legislative and judiciary branches of the regime. It gathers information and creates files regarding these officials.

In all these three branches of the IRGC's Intelligence Organization, all reports are gathered through Bassij operatives, who identify and consistently monitor their targets.

The Guardian Council's supervisors or observers in every city and province are in constant contact with the IRGC Intelligence Organization's political office based in their respective cities and provinces. Therefore, following the registration of candidates, the IRGC's Intelligence Organization delivers recommendations and the candidates' files to Guardian Council observers. Disqualifications are done on the basis of these recommendations.

Files on regime officials contain all of their voting records, speeches, and letters signed while in parliament, among other things. They are disqualified after evidence is presented about incongruities and inconsistencies with Khamenei's positions and guidelines.

The Purge and Disqualifications by the Guardian Council in the Current Parliamentary Election

For the 10th round of elections for the 290-seat parliament, held on February 26, 2016, 12,123 people registered. The Guardian Council's

Supervisory Office announced the results of its initial reviews on January 18, 2016. The table below outlines the results:

Total # of Candidates	# of Withdrawn Candidacies	No. of Disqualifications	Inconclusive	Approvals	% of Approvals
12,039	516	3,276	3,525	4,722	39.22

As can be noted from the table above, the supervisory body has approved only about 40 percent of the candidates while the remaining 60 percent were dismissed in two categories: disqualified or inconclusive. The 60 percent were from the so-called "reformist" faction, supporters of the Rouhani government and some Principalists close to Ali Larijani.

On January 18, 2016, the state-affiliated Fars news agency reported that among the disqualified are 37 former parliament deputies (9th session) whose candidacies were rejected by electoral supervisory bodies. 25 were Principalists, 8 reformists, and 4 independents. Supporters of Larijani were especially those who backed the nuclear deal and who signed declarations that were implicitly although indirectly against Khamenei.

On January 31, 2016, Fars reported: "Ebrahimian, a jurist member of the Guardian Council has announced that about 6,000 candidates of the tenth round of the parliamentary elections have appealed the supervisory office's decision and their cases are being reviewed. They said that a large number of these 6,000 candidates for the tenth parliamentary election do not comply with the two conditions of practical allegiance to Islam and the *velayat-e faqih*, in accordance with Article 28 of the electoral law."

After extensive protests and feuds with eliminated factions, the regime found itself-- weakened in its entirety and extremely weary of social protests (a red line). Subsequently, the Guardian Council embarked on a clear retreat on February 6, 2016, announcing that an additional 15 percent of the candidates had been approved, bringing and the total number of those approved to 55 percent of the entire field.

This about-face was orchestrated by the Khamenei faction, which in a tactical move initially engaged in wholesale disqualifications, allowing it to then back down to give the appearance of making "concessions" to rival factions.

All Candidates and Disqualifications in 31 Provinces for the 10th Parliamentary Elections

Source: Fars news agency, February 7, 2016

No.	Province	Registered	Withdrawals	Approved
1	Eastern Azarbaijan	623	31	363
2	Western Azarbaijan	444	21	179
3	Ardebil	203	16	123
4	Isfahan	1015	48	185
5	Alborz	281	5	81

6	Ilam	108	3	46
7	Boushehr	110	5	53
8	Tehran	2734	33	1144
9	Charmahal-va-Bakhtiari	146	26	74
10	Southern Khorassan	102	5	60
11	Khorassan Razavi	854	21	561
12	Northern Khorassan	95	3	61
13	Khouzestan	623	18	361
14	Zanjan	187	3	105
15	Semnan	109	7	63
16	Sistan-va-Balouchestan	299	14	126
17	Fars	727	47	180
18	Qazvin	153	6	83
19	Qom	161	10	93
20	Kurdistan	213	5	100
21	Kerman	267	16	143

22	Kermanshah	295	14	92
23	Kohkilouyeh-va-Boyerahmad	108	4	71
24	Golestan	305	14	148
25	Gilan	367	20	196
26	Lorestan	307	7	172
27	Mazandaran	305	13	169
28	Markazi	334		183
29	Hormozgan	101	12	41
30	Hamedan	297	9	201
31	Yazd	172	4	100

Past Disqualifications by the Guardian Council for Parliamentary Elections

Session	Registered	Approved	Disqualified/Inconclusive	% Approved
First	3694	1850	1844	50.08
Second	1592	1275	317	80.09
Third	1999	1666	333	83.34
Fourth	3233	2970	263	91.87

Fifth	8365	2929	5436	35.01
Sixth	6835	5083	1752	74.37
Seventh	8174	4465	3709	54.62
Eighth	7595	4500	3095	59.25
Ninth	5382	3369	2013	62.6
Tenth	12032	4722	7310	39.25

Past Disqualifications Chart by the Guardian Council for Parliamentary Elections

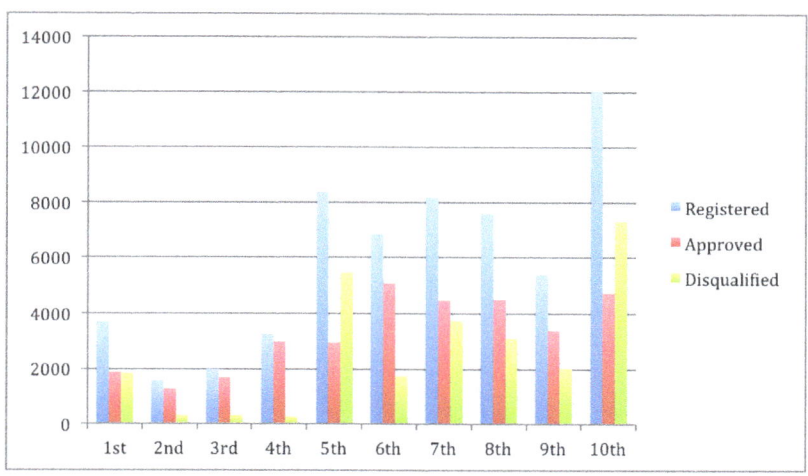

Notes:

- The first session of parliament took place after the anti-monarchical revolution in 1979, when the Interior Ministry was essentially in charge of disqualifying candidates. That round of elections was different in this respect from the subsequent 9 sessions, for which the Guardian Council took over that responsibility.

- The second and third sessions of parliament were during the time that Khomeini was the supreme leader and the Guardian Council's disqualifications were limited (essentially disqualifying members of the *Nehzat-e Azadi* or Freedom Movement party).

- The fourth session was during a period of open alliance between Khamenei and Rafsanjani against the faction of "Followers of Imam's Line." The latter faction refused to participate in elections in protest to the "Approbation Supervision" principle that was instituted at that time, and that is why the number of disqualifications is lower.

- The fifth session took place when a feud broke out between Rafsanjani and Khamenei. Khamenei attempted to sideline the Rafsanjani faction ("Kargozaran" or the Construction Party), which had forged an alliance with the Followers of the Imam's Line. Supporters of the latter faction were very active during this period, which explains why the highest number of disqualifications happened during this time (65 percent).

- The sixth round of parliamentary elections took place after the revelation of the chain murders of intellectuals and activists, which led to the weakening of the Khamenei faction, and when Rafsanjani personally entered the race.

Hence, the Guardian Council, despite its intentions, could not disqualify more than 25 percent of the candidates.

- During the seventh, eighth and ninth sessions, so-called reformists were essentially rejected. Khamenei succeeded in organizing a favourable parliament for himself for the seventh session, which had his ally Haddad Adel as its speaker. But, the eight and ninth sessions of the parliament witnessed fissures within Khamenei's own faction, which led to Ali Larijani becoming speaker counter to Khamenei's preference. (Larijani heads a more moderate faction of pro-Khamenei elements.)

Election Funding and the Illicit Role of the Iranian Regime's Organizations

Using Drug Money to Pay for Campaigns

The regime's array of security and intelligence organizations, including the IRGC, play a significant role in covering election costs, including campaign ads, vote-buying, paying their own agents, perks, financial incentives and other measures. The majority of election costs for the regime's internal factions are paid out of profits from drug smuggling, theft, and skimming. Below are a number of confessions by the regime's own officials in this regard:

- In early 2015, the regime's Interior Minister, Rahmani Fazli, said that a "portion of the drug money has entered the political sphere and is being spent in the context of helping candidates in elections and facilitating decision making."

- The spokesman of the parliament chairing committee, Behrouz Nemati, said on April 20, 2015, "At today's parliamentary chairing committee, topics related to the subject of dirty money were discussed and it has been directed that Mr. Rahmani Fazli produce a report to deputies at an open session of the parliament regarding the issue of dirty money."

- On April 20, 2015, a member of parliament from Khoi talked about the creation of campaigns by certain people whose wealth had been attained through activities like smuggling, excess profits from imports of pharmaceutical drugs or special permission to sell foreign currencies under the previous government. He added, "The brother of the same person who had given some money to Mr. Rahimi and is now in prison has now set up a campaign office. Another example is a man who was involved in illegal smuggling and who now runs a branch of a charity organization. He is using that as a cover to carry out extensive activities regarding elections. They lie that they are performing charity work. I know someone who is a former official and is now extremely rich and has created a vast campaign network."

- On November 19, 2015, Mohammad-Hossein Moqimi, head of the national Elections Committee, said, "Monies attained from sources involved in money laundering, illicit activities and drugs cannot be used to pay for expenses incurred during election campaigns. Currently, funds obtained from drug smuggling enter the market and are spent in various spheres, including the electoral process."

- On January 23, 2016, Valiollah Seyf, head of the Iranian Central Bank, announced that the Central Bank had begun efforts to identify and prevent the use of "dirty money" in the upcoming elections.

- The minister of justice, Mostafa Pourmohammadi, said, "It is not legal for illicit, immoral, and unjust money to be used in elections. We are seeking to control these costs. But one should not publicize the discussions about dirty money in the media, public opinion or other places."

- A website tied to former IRGC commander Mohsen Rezai, *Tabnak*, reported on January 31, 2016: "13 parliamentary deputies have written a letter to Rouhani saying: These days we are witnessing a swelling in the ranks of protestors who had invested in an illegal company called Thamen al-Hojaj, gathering in front of the parliament and the Central Bank. Your campaign headquarters in 2013 was located in the main building of the Thamen al-Hojaj company - situated on Karimkhan Street just before Haft-e Tir Square. There was a relationship between this illegal company and your campaign headquarters, and there was a relationship between people's investments in that company and your election expenses. None of the company officials have been held to account. These facts have raised many suspicions among the public, especially those who invested and lost their money in this company. Therefore, we ask that you clarify, in a transparent and public manner, this suspicious relationship between your campaign expenses and the lost investments of people in the Thamen al-Hojaj company."

Political Parties within the Regime

Statistics and Political Affiliations of Candidates and Disqualifications by the Guardian Council

According to the table below, only one percent of the "reformists" were approved in the first round of disqualifications (not finalized)

Party Name	Faction	# of Candidates	# of Approvals
National Trust (Etemad Melli)	Reformist	54	1
Construction (Kargozaran)	Reformist	100	0
Islamic Association of University Instructors	Reformist	7	0
Moderation and Development	Rouhani	340	40
Islamic Association of Iranian Medical Society	Reformist	26	0
Iranian Nation Party	Reformist	146	0

Will of the Iranian Nation Party	Reformist	6	0
Society of Developers (Abadgaran)	Principalists	1	1
Islamic Coalition Party (Motalefeh)	Principalists	290	290
Society of the Loyalists of the Islamic Revolution (Vafadaran)	Principalists	3	3
Democracy Party (Mardomsalari)	Reformist	60	10
Solidarity of Iranian Graduates	Reformist	8	0
Solidarity Party (Hambastegi)	Reformist	12	0

The "Reformist" Faction and Its Electoral Tactics

No.	Party Name	Founding Date	Secretary General	Organ	Comments
1	Islamic Iran Unity and Cooperation	2012	Mohammad-Reza Chamani		
2	Voice of Iranians Party	2014	Majid Farahani		Chairman of the central council is Sadeq Kharrazi
3	Aref Spectrum		Mohammad-Reza Aref	Reformist groups	Coordination to produce a unified list
4	Islamic Iran National Unity	2015	Shoja Pourian		The party has been formed by some of the members of the Participation Front
5	National Trust (Etemad-e Melli)	2005	Has not had a central committee and secretary general since 2010	United reformists	Personalities include Rasoul Montakhabnia and Elias Hazrati
6	Construction (Kargozaran)	1995	Gholam-Hossein Karbaschi	Formed by some of the former Rafsanjani cabinet members	Spokesman is Hossein Marashi

7	Coordination Council of Reformist Coalition		Farajollah Kamijani (acting chair)	Secretary general of Islamic Educators Society	
8	Association of Combatant Clerics		Mohammad Moussavi Khoiniha	Split from the Combatant Clergy Association	Members include Seyyed Hadi Khamenei and Hadi Ghaffari
9	Imam Line Forces Association	1998	Seyyed Hadi Khamenei		
10	Democracy Party	2000	Mostafa Kavakabian	Main daily is the Mardomsalari newspaper	
11	Workers' Home	1979	Alireza Mahjoub		
12	Islamic Iran Solidarity	1997	Ali-Asqar Ahmadi	Main daily is the Hambastegi	

The so-called "reformists" registered in large numbers for the 2016 elections. They can be categorized into three groups:
1) Well-known figures,
2) Less-known figures, and
3) An unknown field of candidates who have committed to working in the context of reformist policies if they are elected.

Except for a handful of people, the Guardian Council essentially rejected everyone from the first category. Half of the second category was also disqualified. As a result, the chair of the reformists' provincial policy-making council, Hossein Marashi, has said that only one percent of "reformists" made it through the initial round of disqualifications. He added that in some provinces there are no reformist candidates or even supporters of the government.

On February 6, 2016, the daily *Iran* wrote about the situation of the reformists after the widespread disqualifications: "On the basis of these disqualifications, reformists have no qualified candidates in six provinces, including Gilan with 13 seats, Lorestan with 9 seats, Kerman with 9 seats, Kermanshah with 8 seats, Charmahal-va-Bakhtiari with four seats and Boushehr with four seats. In most other electoral districts, at least in a statistical sense, the number of approved reformist, moderate or independent candidates are drastically lower than their principalist rivals."

Despite the purges carried out by the Guardian Council, currently the reformists' policy is to not boycott the elections or refuse to participate. They are instead lodging a large number of complaints and appeals, while publicizing the fact that the disqualifications were made on political grounds. Next, once the approvals and disqualifications have been finalized, they will create a list of people in the other two categories, with those who are disqualified announcing that they will back the third category (the unknown field of candidates).

The Rafsanjani-Rouhani and reformist factions relied on two tactics in order to confront the disqualifications: First, a public relations campaign against the Guardian Council (with Rafsanjani and Rouhani leading the charge), in order to dull the sharp edges of the Guardian Council's actions as much as possible. Second, they promoted a number of youth supporting this faction and presented female candidates (publicizing the slogan "30 percent of parliament belongs to women"), in order to cause problems for the Guardian Council both in terms of identifying the candidates and also rejecting them.

The pro-Rafsanjani camp is using youth and women as a political instrument to overcome the hegemonic ambitions of the rival pro-Khamenei faction. Were it not for the "elections" and its need to acquire more influence, it would not have resorted to such tactics. Indeed, Rafsanjani's extremely misogynist comments about the inferior size of women's brains, among other statements, are well known in Iranian society. Similarly, Iranian youth remember that during the July 1999 student uprisings, Rouhani vehemently called for the suppression of the protests that violated "Islam," and the principle of *velayat-e faqih* (absolute clerical rule). So, this recent tactic of their factions should not be seen as a genuine stab at inclusion and expansion of the circle of participants in elections. It is simply a ploy to grab more seats and access to the financial resources the regime has monopolized for the past 37 years.

The "Principalists" (pro-Khamenei) Faction and Electoral Tactics

No.	Party Name	Founding Date	Secretary General	Organ	Comments
1	Society of Seminary Teachers	1961	Ayatollah Mohammad Yazdi		
2	Society of Devotees of the Islamic Revolution (Isargaran)	1997	Founders: Hossein Fadai, Ali Akbar Torabifard and Darabi		
3	Perseverance Front of Islamic Iran (Istadegi)	2010	Yadollah Habibi	Founder: Mohsen Rezai	Tied to Principalists factions and organizations

4	Islamic Iran Coalition of Development and Justice	2013	Qorbanzadeh	Previous SG: Morteza Talai, with central influence from Mohammad-Baqer Qalibaf	
5	Velayat Followers Parliamentary Group	2012	Kazem Jalali	170 members of parliament belong to the Velayat faction in parliament	
6	Perseverance Coalition (Paydari)	2011	Morteza Aqa Tehrani	Weekly 9-Dey	
7	Ahmadinejad Supporters (Homa)	2015		Network of governors and managers during Ahmadinejad's 8-year tenure	A circle of people close to former president Mahmoud Ahmadinejad; On April 19, 2015, 60 former public sector managers met in Shiraz

8	Y.E.K.T.A. Coalition	2015	Hamid-Reza Hajbabai		Founders: Fereydoun Abbas Davani, Mohammad Mehdi Zahedi, Hamid-Reza Hajbabai, Kamran Daneshjou, Seyyed Mohammad Hosseini, Mohammad-Hassan Tariqat Monfared, Massoud Zaribafan, Mohammad Abbasi, Lotfollah Forouzandeh, Alireza Ali Ahmadi, Ebrahim Azizi, Asadollah Abbasi
9	Followers of the Islamic Revolution Society (Rahpouyan)		Parviz Sarvari, deputy		
10	Followers of the Line of Imam and the Leader		Mohammad-Reza Bahonar		

11	Popular Defenders of National Integrity Party		Mortezairad (spokesman)		
12	Islamic Coalition Party (Motalefeh)		Mohammad-Nabi Habibi		Asadollah Badamchian, deputy

Following the signing of the nuclear agreement between world powers and Tehran in 2015, the Principalists affiliated with Khamenei witnessed splits and fissures in their ranks. The Islamic Coalition faction or *Motalefeh*, which had traditionally advocated centralist positions (vacillating between Rafsanjani and Khamenei), is now allied with the more extremist *Delvapasan* faction (the Perseverance Front and mullah Mesbah Yazdi, who supported Mahmoud Ahmadinejad previously).

The Combatant Clergy Association, which until the death of Mahdavi Kani in 2014 also adopted centralist positions between those of Rafsanjani and Khamenei, is now under the leadership of Movahedi Kermani inching towards the Society of Seminary Teachers and Mesbah Yazdi (against Rafsanjani).

Ali Larijani, who used to be the head of the traditional Principalists faction, is now comparatively closer to Rafsanjani alongside figures like Nateq Nouri and Ali Akbar Velayati (they are still considered Principalists but closer to the positions of the Hassan Rouhani faction).

The central policy of Khamenei's faction is to disqualify rival factions through the Guardian Council. By relying on slogans such as preventing the "penetration" of foreigners after the nuclear deal and preventing the rise of agents of "sedition" (those tied to the 2009 uprisings), the unfavourable candidates are being identified by the IRGC and later disqualified by the Guardian Council. In the face of the onslaught of rival factions, the IRGC and the pro-Khamenei factions are intent on preserving their hold on the vast economic power and financial resources that they have attained over the past few decades.

Misogyny in the parliament

Participation of Women

Statistics on the participation of women in the regime's parliamentary elections clearly unmask the misogynist nature of the theocracy. Under the clerical regime's constitution, women are not allowed to run for president and are barred from becoming judges, not to mention not even having freedom of choice when it comes to choosing their own clothing. In a word, women in Iran are legally considered second-class citizens. It is little wonder that young women demanding gender equality have led many social protests and national uprisings, like the 2009 uprising.

As indicated in the table below, the number of female registered candidates in the last nine elections was less than 3 percent.

Just as a growing participation among women in parliament and governance of democratic societies is a barometer of the advancement of democracy in those countries, in the misogynist *velayat-e faqih* regime the low numbers on female participation are indicative of the degree of suppression and dictatorship in Iran.

The current parliament has 9 female deputies among 290 (roughly 3 percent). According to the World Bank's 2015 statistics, on this benchmark, Iran is ranked 134 out of 190 counties, alongside Brazil and Lebanon.

Table - Number of Women in the Regime's Parliaments

Session	First	Second	Third	Fourth	Fifth	Sixth	Seventh	Eighth	Ninth
Number of women	4	4	4	9	14	13	13	8	9
% of women	1.5%	1.5%	1.5%	3.4%	4.8%	4.5%	4.5%	2.8%	3.10%

Chapter 2: Analysis of the 2016 Elections

Engineering of Election Results by Khamenei

- *Khamenei's plans for preserving a majority by the Principalists while sidelining candidates from the Ahmadinejad and reformist factions;*
- *Khamenei's insistence on the active participation of the IRGC in electoral affairs*
- *Decisions by the regime's Supreme National Security Council aimed at preventing popular uprisings and handing over security matters to the IRGC until June 2016*

Background

Contrary to the regime's claims that the people elect its officials, the medieval structure of the *velayat-e faqih* (absolute clerical rule) system is essentially contradictory to any form of election or popular vote. The clerical regime has since the beginning pursued an "Islamic State," with a caliph who in the words of Khomeini should be able to "cut hands, gouge out eyes, and carry out punishments."

But the anti-monarchical revolution of the Iranian people in 1979, which had "freedom" as its main slogan, imposed the concept of elections on Khomeini who would have otherwise sought to establish a truly medieval "caliphate." Therefore, the Iranian people, especially women, and the Iranian Resistance have consistently boycotted the Iranian regime's sham elections after the first round of parliamentary and presidential elections.

Engineering of election results by the Supreme Leader

At the same time, the Iranian people continue to welcome the expansion and deepening of the regime's internal power struggle and feuds, in the belief that they will damage the entire edifice and create opportunities and space wherein blows to the inhuman regime can hasten its downfall, and consequently the establishment of democracy and freedom for the Iranian people. That is why internal feuds and contradictions, and by extension the elections of the regime, are closely watched and analyzed.

Over the past 37 years, the regime has consistently experienced contradictions and infighting at the highest echelons of power. The parliamentary elections are used as a means to grab more power, suppress the population and usurp more wealth. They have also been an appropriate forum to settle internal scores. But the regime's infighting is different in the 2016 elections, for several important reasons:

- The supreme leader's authority was significantly undermined after the 2009 national uprisings
- Key socio-economic and political crises after the institution of international sanctions since 2011 are having an impact inside the country
- Khamenei feared another uprising similar to the one that took place in 2009 and allowed the presidency of Rouhani in 2013, which created bipolarity within the regime.

The results of these defeats let to the acceptance of the nuclear deal, which effectively means that the regime has taken the poison pill. Therefore, it can be concluded that following the nuclear deal, the clerical regime has been weakened in its entirety, in all dimensions of its power, including domestic, regional and international, facing intractable crises. In sum, this "existential" crisis will in all probability lead to its ultimate overthrow.

In such circumstances, rival factions are not advocates of reform, democracy or moderation. They are simply trying to demand their share of power in an undemocratic and unpopular system. In 2016, the weaker factions of Rafsanjani and Rouhani prepared themselves to use the Assembly of Experts elections to bring in a larger number of clerical allies, creating an albeit limited block that could still put a dent in Khamenei's hegemony within the regime. They also sought a majority in parliament so that it would back legislation favourable to the Rafsanjani-Rouhani policies.

However, Khamenei will use all the tools and resources at his disposal to prevent the further deterioration of his hegemony and authority.

Therefore, whatever the outcome of these elections, whether Khamenei acquiesces to a parliament with a limited Rafsanjani hegemony or whether, like in 2009, he intends to exclusively promote his own faction, the post-election environment will usher in a new and more vulnerable phase for the regime.

Reasons for Escalation of Infighting on the Brink of the Elections

Following the nuclear agreement and the regime's retreat, the theocracy in its entirety has become much weaker, which explains why this round of elections for parliament and the Assembly of Experts has greater significance for the two poles of the regime (Khamenei and Rafsanjani). Despite the fact that they both share fundamentally similar socio-political roots and policies, they have disagreements when it comes to the methods and solutions for overcoming the crises of overthrow and preserving the regime.

Khamenei and his faction rely on the IRGC and the security-intelligence apparatus to increase domestic suppression and step up foreign terrorism, helping them to keep the significant economic and financial capital that they have amassed. The Rouhani-Rafsanjani faction, on the other hand, are fearful of the inevitable social uprisings following the nuclear agreement, and therefore seek to continue that trend with further retreats in foreign policy and reductions in their reliance on hard power. They seek to take away some of the IRGC's economic prowess to make room for the realization of their own economic ambitions.

By using the Guardian Council and the leverage of disqualifications, Khamenei wants to prevent the further deterioration of his hegemony in parliament and the Assembly of Experts. That explains why so far in 2016, the Guardian Council's disqualifications, based on intelligence and information provided by the IRGC ("reports from the faithful"), have been considerable and extensive.

Rafsanjani-Rouhani Take Their Fight to the Guardian Council

For their part, Rafsanjani, Rouhani and the so-called "reformist" camp are fighting the disqualifications and inevitable electoral fraud by, on the one hand, publicizing the illegal aspects of the Guardian Council's actions while on the other hand introducing a number of youth and well-known local personalities to enable them to jump over the Guardian Council hurdle. At the same time, they are also warning Khamenei about the ramifications of disqualifications and electoral fraud, which they say could lead to social uprisings and protests!

At times, the increasing levels of internal feuds burst into the state-run media. Below are some examples:

1. On August 19, 2015, Rouhani told a gathering of central and provincial government officials: "The next Islamic Consultative Assembly (parliament) will not belong to only one party or faction. Is it possible for any one faction to say, I have found a solution, which I will use to dye the entire place with my favourite colour? It shouldn't be like that. The esteemed Guardian Council is a monitoring body, not an executive body. The electoral executive body is the government. The government is responsible for organizing elections while another body has been tasked with monitoring elections to ensure illegal activities do not occur. The Guardian Council is the metaphorical eye, and an eye cannot do the job of a hand. Therefore, the separate functions of monitoring and execution must not be conflated."

2. But less than a month later, On September 9, 2015, Khamenei undermined Rouhani's comments and said: "There are some inside the country who in an erroneous manner undercut the health of elections and even before the elections have taken place, they are talking about fraud and are expressing concerns about irregularities. Why are these people expressing misplaced concerns and irrational warnings that undermine (public) trust? What is the real intent behind repeating such statements? The Guardian Council is the watchful eye of the system during the elections and the supervisory role of the Guardian Council during elections is approbatory and impactful."

3. On February 1, 2016, Rafsanjani spoke on the occasion of Khomeini's return from Paris to Tehran in 1979. Speaking at the Mehrabad International Airport's Terminal 1, he issued a veiled threat to the Guardian Council and Khamenei, saying: "Where did you get your own qualifications? Who allowed you to judge? Who allowed you to sit somewhere and act as the arbiter? Who allowed you to gain authority over the parliament, government in addition to other powers? Who allowed you to have control over weapons and public forums? Who allowed you to have control over Friday prayers and the state-run broadcaster? Who granted you these things?"

4. On January 30, 2016, Rafsanjani reacted to the wholesale disqualifications of reformists and government supporters and said: "The vetting process for candidates should not be insurmountable for some and easy and smooth for others."

Reports obtained from inside the regime indicate that internal feuds after the conclusion of the nuclear agreement have intensified. The intent behind these rivalries is to gain more parliamentary and Assembly of Experts seats. A large number of sessions have been organized to discuss ways of eliminating rival factions:

On February 20, 2015, an IRGC official said at a briefing session with the guards: "Rouhani and Rafsanjani won't be able to do much in the Assembly of Experts. In the next parliament, reformists will not have a unified list and they will be hurt. Today, the IRGC's intelligence organization is working on these camps to deepen divisions among them."

On August 6, 2015, a former Ahmadinejad cabinet minister said: "Rafsanjani's main goal is to win the elections and align the executive and legislative branches more closely. They believe that parliament is slowing down the progress being made by the government. Their maximalist position is to gain complete victory in parliamentary elections. Their minimalist desire is a neutral parliament like the seventh session that would give the government more room to manoeuvre. Of course, the main target of Rafsanjani and Rouhani is the Assembly of Experts where they seek an acceptable majority that would enable them to pick the chairman, but they won't succeed."

On June 22, 2015, a pro-Rafsanjani member of the Exigency Council said: "If we succeed in empowering a rational bloc, even if that means rational principalists, there will be domestic and regional stability. These escapades, through which principalists and *Delvapasan* want to flex their muscles, will not happen and such groups will not find the opportunity to act. Even now, we are feeling the pain of such adventures and mismanagement over the eight years that they were in power, in domestic and regional terms. Principalists like Kouchakzadeh, Rasai and Qoddusi certainly know that if such a trend continues, and if the atmosphere of elections is positive, they will not have enough votes and they will not maintain their majority."

On October 29, 2015, one of the pro-Rafsanjani Interior Ministry officials said: "Following the nuclear agreement, the Principalists have become more irritated, adopting a harder line. In some recent meetings, they are even criticizing Khamenei, saying that Khamenei is talking with both sides of his mouth. Khamenei intends to strike a balance between the two rival factions. To compensate for the concession he gave to the reformists regarding the nuclear agreement, he now wants to give concessions to the *Delvapasan* faction and his own supporters. So, the Guardian Council will be serious in the disqualifications of the reformists and will not allow them to enter the parliament and the Assembly of experts, so that the next parliament can be controlled by the Principalists."

On November 22, 2015, one of the pro-Rafsanjani officials of the Elections Committee said: "Rafsanjani is trying to pre-emptively neutralize the Guardian Council by imposing pressures. By registering for the elections, he will once again create a buzz in the media and among personalities against the Guardian Council, thereby affecting public opinion. So, regardless of who is qualified or disqualified, this pressure will create an atmosphere for the elections whereby it can restrain the Guardian Council."

Khamenei Personally Manipulates Elections

On the basis of confidential documents obtained by the Iranian Resistance from inside the regime, in addition to the factional feuding at the lower levels of the regime, Khamenei has for some time been designing a plan to engineer the elections, which he has already implemented. According to this plan, the Principalists must maintain a majority in parliament and the IRGC must enter the elections with all its resources.

Khamenei has two main objectives for engineering the results. First, that the Principalists (his own faction) must be able to keep their majority in parliament. Second, any threat of uprising or social protest, which remains a red line for the regime, must be averted. In this light, the level of popular participation is not as important because the regime can engineer the results. Some of the evidence for these claims is provided below.

Ruhollah Khomeini's grandson at center of controversy

Excerpts of a confidential report produced by Khamenei's office: "In late December 2015, His Excellency (Khamenei) met privately with Ayatollah Jannati, chairman of the Guardian Council, with respect to the elections. Subsequent to this meeting, Ayatollah Jannati held several meetings in the presence of some members of the supreme leader's office, including Mohammadi Golpayegani (Khamenei's chief of staff), Mohammad-Ali Jafari (commander of the IRGC), Mohsen Kazemeini (commander of the IRGC in Tehran), and Mohammad-Reza Naqdi (commander of the Bassij Force), about engineering the elections and Guardian Council's methods in vetting candidates. In accordance with the guidelines mandated by His Excellency, it was decided in these meetings that both the reformists and some of the people close to Ahmadinejad should have the least number of candidates participating in the elections. A final list was produced at the end of the meetings. The qualification of Seyyed Hassan Khomeini (Khomeini's grandson) has not been approved in the Guardian Council or the IRGC. The issue of his qualification was escalated to His Excellency. In the course of these meetings, the qualification of Hassan Khomeini in the elections of the Assembly of Experts was rejected. Subsequently, after contacting the supreme leader's office, and in view of the potential dangers of this measure, on the basis of necessity and the supreme leader's opinions, the candidacy of Rouhani was approved to stand for elections. The candidacy of Rafsanjani was also approved. Those present in the meeting also discussed the implications of the widespread disqualifications and concluded that the least of these threats is a boycott of the elections by the people. Vahid brought a message from His Excellency saying that we should stay on course, and just as His Excellency supported us during the seventh round of parliamentary elections, he will also defend us this time around.

"The esteemed attendees at the meeting were worried more about the security situation than the level of popular participation in the elections. Commander Jafari insisted that the level of popular participation is only a matter of stats and figures that can be adjusted as needed. There is precedent for this in all previous elections, and the rate of participation has been announced, as needed, at higher levels. The Guardian Council has permitted this practice on Sharia grounds."

IRGC commander Mohammad Ali Jafari

In December 2015, Khamenei met with senior IRGC commanders and IRGC commanders on the ground in Syria. In the meeting, after reviewing the latest developments and reasons for the IRGC's defeat in Syria's Aleppo region, Khamenei talked about the upcoming parliamentary and Assembly of Experts elections, saying: "The IRGC's role is to guard the revolution. And in this sensitive juncture, the IRGC's officials and commanders must enter the scene of the elections in whatever way they deem would guard the revolution. The IRGC has a serious role in all spheres and in elections, too, it must play an equal role so that the ploys of penetrators and those who have deviated can be neutralized."

The IRGC and the Intelligence Ministry have already made the decisions. In the latter part of January 2016, when the review of candidate qualifications was apparently under way, an internal Guardian Council report reads: "The Intelligence Ministry and the IRGC communicated a list of favourable candidates to the Guardian Council. The list was also reviewed in a joint session with the esteemed chairman of the Guardian Council and the names were once again vetted."

In late December 2015, the Guardian Council sent a confidential memo to several members of the central council of the Society of Seminary Teachers, which reads: "After the passing of Ayatollah Mahdavi Kani, the first goal of the coalition of those who have diverted from the path of the revolution was to gain dominance over the Assembly of Experts' chairing committee through Rafsanjani. This new sedition was neutralized thanks to the utter vigilance and unity of the Principalists, and Rafsanjani was defeated. The coalition of deviants and agents of foreigners has been meeting for several months, devising plans, and brainstorming. They want to know how they can take over the fifth Assembly of Experts in order to divert the revolution from its main path and obstruct His Excellency (Khamenei). All of the efforts of this coalition are geared towards taking over the Assembly of Experts. As before, they do not care much for parliament.

"The coalition of the deviants led by Rafsanjani, which also has Rouhani and Hassan Khomeini as its figureheads, has made this period into a sensitive juncture. For some time now, they have publicized the topic of a replacement for His Excellency in their domestic and foreign media outlets. They want to show that the fifth session of the Assembly of Experts is sensitive. We must not get caught in the Rafsanjani faction's trap: If such news were to spread in society, the number of the deviants participating in the elections would rise and their hopes for victory would become greater.

"Of course, the Guardian Council will not under any circumstances allow the Assembly of Experts to become dominated by western-minded individuals and the founders of modern aristocracy. If it weren't for the recommendations of the supreme leader's office, we would not have approved the candidacy of Rafsanjani, as we had rejected him during the previous presidential elections. There are particular reasons that will render the vetting process in this period stricter. The Guardian Council will not allow the founders of aristocracy to step into the Assembly of Experts."

In late January 2016, Khamenei sent a message, through a member of his office, to the Principalists, stressing: "The principalist composition of the parliament must be maintained at all costs. Meetings must be held with all principalist parties and groups to share ideas and increase cooperation. Individuals and organizations of the Principalists must refrain from any statements that might sow divisions. The current composition of the parliament, with a majority of Principalists, must be maintained and kept in all circumstances. During these sensitive times, the parliament must belong to revolutionary Principalists."

On November 22, 2015, an IRGC commander said in an internal meeting of the IRGC: "The main thing is the number of seats and asking for more of their share so they can later influence decisions.

The atmosphere might be a little difficult for people like Rafsanjani. So, they will work on other people in the hopes of bringing them to their own side. They are talking about a 20% share in the Assembly of Experts. Of course, the Guardian Council and the supreme leader's office will work to decrease that 20% share. In Tehran, it has been agreed that the Tehran city election executive committees will vet candidates for parliament, who should be picked from among the revolutionary principalists. Issa Farhadi, the governor of Tehran, will be the head of the executive committee of elections in Tehran city."

Meeting of IRGC Commanders on Engineering Election Results

Fear of Popular Protests: Main Factor Behind the Regime's Decisions for Upcoming Elections

In November 2015, IRGC commanders in Tehran held a meeting to review threats during elections. In one of these meetings, one of the IRGC deputies told the attendees: "A number of people close to the president are saying that the Bassij and the IRGC should not take part in the elections. This is while the duty and mission of the IRGC in defending the Islamic revolution is not by military means alone. We have told Rouhani himself to remind his allies that the IRGC will intervene and get involved in whatever sphere it sees necessary to protecting the system and the revolution, let alone important issues like the elections of the Assembly of Experts and parliament, where the IRGC is not looking for anyone's permission to intervene. Now our own country's president is saying that the IRGC should not intervene in elections?! The IRGC launched its electoral activities two months ago, so that it can eliminate those who deviate from the positions of the supreme leader. After the 2009 elections (uprisings), it was the IRGC that saved the country. And during the upcoming elections, too, the IRGC will intervene with all its might, and it will continue to do so."

Decisions by the Supreme National Security Council on the Eve of the Elections

In December 2015, the regime's Supreme National Security Council held a session entitled "Lessons from the 2009 Sedition: Vigilance and Preparations in the Current Circumstances," where participants reviewed the security situation for the upcoming elections. The participants referred to the 2009 uprisings and pointed to the fact that the regime's organizations were astonished and surprised by the social protests. They added that this time around, too, anything is possible and a large occurrence might take place with a spark. Therefore, vigilance and preparations are required to prevent "chaos," even if the probability of such an occurrence is one percent. Subsequent to this review, the following decisions were adopted:

From December 2015 to June 2016, Tehran's security portfolio would be completely handed over to the IRGC's Sarollah Corps. Tehran has been divided into 65 security zones with one specific IRGC unit in charge of each of these zones. A central war room has been set up to control the overall security. This central operations control room includes the IRGC commander of Tehran province, the Intelligence Minister, the commander of the State Security Forces, the Interior Minister, the Tehran governor, and the Deputy Interior Minister for political and security affairs. All of the police and State Security Forces have been placed under the command of this war room, with the IRGC commanding it. For the next six months, more than 160,000 forces have been assigned to secure the capital. The security of all other provinces and large cities has also been handed over to the IRGC, with the State Security Forces, and the intelligence and security organs placed under the command of the IRGC in those provinces. According to the Supreme National Security Council resolution, to compensate for the lack of sufficient forces, the regime will use Iraqi and Yemeni militias tied to the Qods Force (the extraterritorial terrorist arm of the IRGC).

On December 19, 2015, the head of the security office of national elections committee, Zolfaghari, said: "The security map of elections has been drawn up. Out of the 207 main electoral districts tied to parliamentary elections, a total of four provinces with 10 electoral districts have been red-flagged on security grounds. We must certainly start working to organize the elections without any problems whatsoever. There are 50 electoral districts flagged as "gray," 22 as "yellow," and 125 as "white."

The Interior Minister talks about the "critical security situation" in 10 electoral districts: On December 20, 2015, Radio Free Europe (*Radio Farda*) reported: According to Abdol-Reza Rahmani Fazli, the Iranian Interior Minister, there are 10 regions in Iran that have a particularly sensitive security situation. They are rated as critical. The Interior Minister pointed to these 10 electoral districts with a "red" status, saying that the reasons for this rating are "the special circumstances of the region," "threats posed by enemies," and "some ethnic feuds that in the past have even led to deaths." He added: There are 10 regions in the entire country that we see as sensitive and we have assigned forces to maintain security in these regions.

On October 15, 2015, one of the State Security Forces experts said: "There is a huge economic burden on the people and even some teachers who have no political demands can have their non-political requests translate into security crises, which would then become political. The state of society is not at all predictable. A small incident can push the society towards crises and security challenges. The tolerance and hopes of people are no longer high. The people have completely lost hope in the government and the system, which is extremely dangerous."

On November 30, 2015, one of the officials of the social department of the State Security Forces wrote in an internal memo: "The main challenge facing society and the upcoming elections is the illegitimacy of the system, which we have lost. We must regain this legitimacy through the elections. We must relieve people of some pressures. We are evaluating nine outcomes with respect to probable threats, each of which can cause a social crisis."

On December 25, 2015, a member of the IRGC's political office said in an internal memo: "With respect to the elections, over the past several years, the most important issue under consideration has been the security of the elections. The main worry of the decision-making body is the security situation during elections. The system itself is grappling with a number of internal disagreements, whose main platform for resolution is the elections. With respect to the elections, (Khamenei) has dictated the policy, saying that the Guardian Council protects the rights of the people and we must not allow deviants to enter the race."

THE 2016 VOTE IN IRAN'S THEOCRACY

AN ANALYSIS OF PARLIAMENTARY & ASSEMBLY OF EXPERTS ELECTIONS

NATIONAL COUNCIL OF RESISTANCE OF IRAN
US REPRESENTATIVE OFFICE

February 16, 2016

THE 2016 VOTE IN IRAN'S THEOCRACY; An analysis of Parliamentary & Assembly of Experts Elections

Copyright © National Council of Resistance of Iran - U.S. Representative Office, 2016.

All rights reserved. No part of this monograph may be used or reproduced in any manner whatsoever without written permission except in the case of brief quotations embodied in articles or reviews.

First published in 2016 by
National Council of Resistance of Iran - U.S. Representative Office (NCRI-US), 1747 Pennsylvania Ave., NW, Suite 1125, Washington, DC 20006

ISBN-10: 0-9904327-9-3
ISBN-13: 978-0-9904327-9-1

Library of Congress Cataloging-in-Publication Data

National Council of Resistance of Iran - U.S. Representative Office.
THE 2016 VOTE IN IRAN'S THEOCRACY; An analysis of Parliamentary & Assembly of Experts Elections

1. Iran-Elections. 2. Internal Politics-Iran. 3. Iran-Foreign relations. 4. Security, International. 5. Rouhani, Hassan.

First Edition: February 2016

Printed in the United States of America

These materials are being distributed by the National Council of Resistance of Iran-U.S. Representative Office. Additional information is on file with the Department of Justice, Washington, D.C.

www.ingramcontent.com/pod-product-compliance
Lightning Source LLC
Chambersburg PA
CBHW040330300426
44113CB00020B/2713